Teenage Alcoholism: Parental Influence and How to Get Rid of Vice

Janice F. Thompson

Table of contents

Chapter 1
Chapter 2
Chapter 3
Chapter 4
Chapter 5

Chapter 1

Vulnerability of teenagers to alcoholism

Parents have severe concerns about teen drinking.
Understanding the risk factors for teen alcohol addiction is essential for successful prevention and, if necessary, early intervention.

Because alcohol is the most accessible and often used drug of abuse among teenagers, it is a big worry for both parents and those who contact teenagers.

American teenagers between the ages of 12 and 17 were assessed to be 9% of current drinkers, indicating they had at least one drink within the previous 30 days.
Risks to one's health and safety, which apply to all people regardless of age or drinking status, are among the main effects of underage drinking.
It's crucial to be aware of the variety of reasons why teenagers use alcohol.

Understanding the risk factors for teen alcohol addiction is essential for successful prevention and, if necessary, early intervention.

Teen Alcohol Abuse Internal Risk Factors

One can distinguish between internal risk factors, which are unique to a person, and external risk factors, which are influenced by the environment in which a teen is growing up.
Although internal risk factors for juvenile alcohol consumption are sometimes more difficult to identify and address, doing so can be the most crucial first step in an effective preventative strategy.

How susceptible a person is to developing substance use problems may depend on specific hereditary characteristics.
Predisposition is the name given to a person's innate propensity to struggle with particular issues.
Unquestionably, there is a genetic component to alcoholism, however, studies have shown that

genes only account for roughly 50% of the chance of developing an alcohol use disease. This suggests that other factors can play a role in keeping a teenager from abusing alcohol even if they are genetically inclined to struggle with teenage alcoholism.

While heredity may have an impact, there are also significant elements that can distinguish between abstinence and alcoholism.

Behavior Types

Teenage alcohol consumption has been predicted by a few early childhood characteristics. Impulsivity, restlessness, aggression, and antisocial tendencies have all been linked to traits that indicate a kid is more likely to consume alcohol and develop alcohol use disorders. The connection between alcohol and impulse control is crucial because someone with great impulse control is more likely to refuse alcohol when it is given or to stop drinking altogether.

To prevent alcohol use disorder, it can be very beneficial to study adolescent and brain development about alcohol use.
Regarding certain behavioral patterns and a potentially elevated risk for teen alcohol consumption, a qualified psychologist or psychiatrist can offer appropriate professional judgment.

Anxiety disorders and ADHD
Teenage drinking and an increased likelihood of developing an alcohol use disorder have been linked to specific mental health conditions.
Higher rates of alcohol misuse and dependency have been associated with attention deficit hyperactivity disorder (ADHD), poor social relationship skills, and conduct disorder.

Alcohol abuse and dependency can cause or result in other psychological problems like anxiety and sadness.
To fully comprehend the connection between alcohol misuse and any particular diagnosis that

your child may have, it is crucial to discuss any worries you may have about teen alcohol usage with a qualified psychiatric specialist.

Trauma

Risk factors for adolescent and adult alcohol abuse include traumatic experiences and child maltreatment.

In contrast to other teenagers, adolescents in treatment for alcohol use disorder report greater rates of reported physical abuse, sexual abuse, violent victimization, and witnessing of violence due to the link between childhood trauma and alcoholism.

According to studies on alcohol and trauma, 13% of adolescents who use alcohol are also diagnosed with PTSD (PTSD).

Positive Attitudes Toward Alcohol

An adolescent may be at risk for alcohol misuse for several reasons, but the most common risk factor is whether or not they have a favorable opinion of alcohol.
The most frequent response to the question "why do teenagers drink alcohol?" is that they believe the perceived benefits outweigh the dangers or potentially negative effects.
This is conceivably the only internal risk factor for juvenile alcohol misuse that can be controlled since proactive education on the risky effects of teen alcohol abuse can alter a teen's perspective of alcohol usage.

For teens to make informed decisions about alcohol use and misuse, they need to hear from reliable adults like their parents, teachers, coaches, and other positive role models.
Teenagers won't have any motivation to decline a drink when it is offered to them if they don't hear clear and frequent warnings about the risks associated with teen alcohol usage.

Teenagers should not drink with their parents since it sends confusing messages to them about alcohol consumption.

Teenagers who have a strong understanding of the risks associated with alcohol use will be more likely to say "no" when they are faced with situations that affect teen alcohol usage, such as peer pressure from other teenagers who are acting irresponsibly.

The best form of prevention is proactive, succinct education about the risks of teen alcohol abuse.

Give your teen the knowledge and tools they require so they can decide what is best for them right now.

Factors at External Risk for Teen Alcohol Abuse

While an individual teen's internal risk factors are unique, their environment has a significant impact on external influences and causes of underage drinking.

The teenage years are crucial for learning, interpreting, and developing a distinct worldview.

Teenage alcohol misuse is more likely to occur if the world around them is continuously emphasizing the negative effects of underage drinking.

To provide the necessary preventive and intervention to modify the message kids are receiving about alcohol use, it is crucial to be aware of the potential external influencers for teen alcohol addiction.

Media Promotion

Alcohol advertising has a big impact on young people's decisions to drink alcohol during their adolescent years.

In the age of digital communication, the effect of underage drinking can come from a variety of sources, including social media and online advertising as well as more conventional media like TV, movies, and music.

There is no denying the link between a teen's desire to drink, their preference for alcohol, and media promotion.

Parents must keep an eye on their teenager's use of social media and potential media exposure.
Research demonstrates that alcohol warning adverts and alcohol counter-promotion can help young adults curb their impulse to drink, proving that advertising and social media need not be enemies.
Make sure the advertising your kid is continuously exposed to in the media and on social media serves to positively reinforce the values you are attempting to teach them.

Family members and parents

A teen's decision to start drinking is heavily influenced by their parent's drinking habits and attitudes about alcohol.
Teenagers' poor decision-making is reinforced when their parents let them drink and alcohol is easily available to them.

53 percent of those who are currently underage drinkers said that alcohol was offered by family and friends when surveyed.

Even if you may be providing a positive role model for your adolescent, you need also make sure that all other family members and close friends are.
Make sure you're sending the right messages about how much alcohol is suitable.
Parents' warnings to their children about the risks of alcohol reduce the likelihood that they will begin drinking throughout adolescence.

Peer Influence

Teenage years are challenging socially, and decision-making abilities are still forming.
Due to this reality, peer pressure has a significant impact on many teenagers' behaviors and decisions.
Social acceptability of drinking among peers increases a teen's likelihood of engaging in

underage drinking, according to studies and statistics on the relationship between peer pressure and alcohol usage.

Peer pressure and teen drinking can influence other dangerous choices like drug usage, driving while intoxicated, aggression, and sexual promiscuity.

Positive peer pressure can stimulate excellent decision-making, such as improved academic performance, whereas negative peer pressure can lead to unsafe decision-making.

Parents must be aware of both the good and bad peer influences their children are exposed to.

Keeping Teen Alcohol Abuse at Bay

Underage drinking poses concerns to one's health and development as well as a higher likelihood of engaging in dangerous behavior or becoming a victim of violent crimes.

To prevent alcohol and drug dependence in maturity, underage drinking must be stopped.

Following are some suggestions for preventing teen drinking:

Maintain an open line of communication with your teenager.

Clearly and consistently communicate the dangers of underage drinking.

By allowing underage drinking or events that encourage underage drinking, do not encourage the use of alcohol.

Observe how your teen uses social media.

Encourage healthy peer relationships and step in when your teen's behavior is being influenced by unhealthy ones.

Consult your child's physician or other healthcare professional about any worries you may have regarding teen alcohol use.

Parents must exercise caution and intelligence.

When you have reason to believe your child is abusing alcohol, it's crucial to follow your gut, keep a tight eye on what they're doing, and realize that their safety comes before their privacy.
You can get support from The Recovery Village's addiction specialists, your child's doctor or a guidance counselor to analyze the situation and decide what actions to take next.

Help is always accessible, so call The Recovery Village to speak with a representative about a thorough and individualized teen alcohol treatment plan that best suits your child's requirements if you believe your teen needs it.

Chapter 2

The developing brain of a teenager

PERCEIVING YOUR PRE-TENDER

Teenagers' brains develop and change as they age.
Children's thinking and behavior are impacted by these brain modifications.

Develop healthy teen brains through positive behavior, thought, and sleep habits.

The fundamentals of teenage brain development

When children are very young, their brains go through a significant growth spurt.
Their brains are already 90–95 percent the size of an adult by the time they turn six.
Although the early years are crucial for brain development, the brain still needs to undergo significant remodeling before it can perform as an adult brain.

Adolescence is a time of intense brain remodeling, which lasts until your child is in their mid-20s.
Age, experience, and puberty-related hormonal changes all affect how the brain changes.

Inside the adolescent mind
The teenage brain experiences significant growth and development during adolescence.
The main adjustment is the "pruning" away of unused connections in your child's gray matter, which is the part of the brain responsible for thought and processing.
Other connections are also strengthened at the same time.
Based on the "use it or lose it" tenet, this is the brain's method of improving efficiency.

The rear of the brain is where the pruning process starts.
The prefrontal cortex, located at the front of the brain, undergoes remodeling last.
The prefrontal cortex, which governs decision-making, gives your child the capacity to

plan, consider the repercussions of actions, solve issues, and restrain impulses.
Even as early adults, this area of the brain continues to change.
Teenagers may use the amygdala more than adults do to make decisions and solve issues since the prefrontal cortex is still maturing.
The amygdala is linked to feelings, irrational behavior, hostility, and instinct.

Have you ever observed that while sometimes your child seems to think and act in ways that are illogical, impetuous, or emotional, other times your child seems to think and act in ways that are quite mature?
These transitions and alterations are explained by the back-to-front development of the brain; adolescents are using developing brains.

creating a strong teen brain
The environment your child grows up in, together with his or her particular brain, affects how your youngster behaves, thinks, and feels.

The brain may become "hard-wired" concerning your child's favored activities and skills, for instance.

The development of a teen's brain depends on how they use their free time.
It is important to consider the variety of interests and experiences your child has, including music, sports, academics, foreign languages, and video games.
How do these affect the type of brain that your child will have as an adult?

You play a significant role in shaping your child's environment.
Your child values you greatly.
Your child's ability to develop a healthy brain will depend on how you raise and influence them.

This is possible by:

promoting constructive behavior

assisting your youngster in getting enough sleep while encouraging sound thinking.

Methods for promoting teen brain growth

Your child may experience any of the following as their brains develop:

select risky behavior or high-risk activities.

express their emotions more strongly and openly and act rashly.

Here are some pointers for promoting good conduct and enhancing favorable brain connections:

Let your child take some healthy risks.
Your child can move closer to independence, explore adult behavior, and develop an independent identity with new and different experiences.

Help your child develop new creative and expressive channels for feelings.
Your youngster may be expressing and managing new emotions.
Many teenagers believe that participating in or enjoying sports, music, writing, or other forms of art are healthy outlets.

With your child, go over decisions step-by-step.
Discuss potential actions your child could take and their likely effects with them.
Encourage your child to compare favorable outcomes or rewards to unfavorable ones.

Use family routines to offer your child's life some order.
These might be based on schedules for work, school, and families.

Give opportunities for negotiating those boundaries as well as boundaries themselves.
Young people require parental and other adult guidance and limit setting.

Offer frequent praise and positive rewards for desirable behavior.
This reinforces connections in your child's brain.

Be a positive role model.
Your behavior will display your youngster the behavior you expect.

Keep in touch with your child.
You should usually keep a watch on your child's pals and activities.
Being open and friendly can help you with this.

Talk with your youngster about their developing brain.
Understanding this vital stage of growth could help your child understand their feelings.
Additionally, it might interest your youngster more in caring for their brain.

Teenagers frequently have strong passions for their hobbies, especially those that allow them to interact with others.

By encouraging your child's interests, activities, and hobbies, you can aid in their skill and confidence development.

Thinking techniques for the development of adolescent brains

During these years, as the brain develops, your child will begin to:

more rational thinking

more complex thought and an awareness that problems aren't always straightforward

more attentive to the emotional cues of others

logically resolve complex problems and approach issues from various angles

gain a clearer understanding of the future.

You can use the following techniques to encourage your child's thinking growth:

Promote empathy.
Discuss your own, your child's, and other people's feelings.
Emphasize that various people have different viewpoints and circumstances.
Reiterate how a single action can have a large impact.

Put a focus on both the short- and long-term effects of actions.
The prefrontal cortex, which controls future thought, is still growing during development.
You may promote your child's prefrontal cortex's healthy growth by having conversations with them about how their activities affect both the present and the future.

Try to speak at your child's comprehension level while maintaining a conversational pace.
You can determine if your child has comprehended essential information by having them describe what they just heard to you in their own words.

Encourage the growth of your child's decision-making and problem-solving abilities.
You and your child could go through a process that involves identifying issues, outlining potential solutions, and thinking about solutions that are acceptable to everyone.
Providing these abilities as role models is also crucial.

teen brain development and sleep

Sleep patterns alter during adolescence as a result of hormonal changes in the brain.
However, kids still require a lot of sleep for their general well-being and development, which includes brain development.

This advice can assist your kid in getting the rest they require:

Make sure your youngster has a peaceful, cozy place to sleep.

Promote "winding down" before bedtime without using any devices, including phones.

Encourage your youngster to follow a consistent schedule for bedtime and waking up.

Encourage your child to sleep for 8 to 10 hours per night.

Chapter 3

Teenagers' growth and development

How much more will adolescence develop me?

Adolescence is another name for the adolescent years.

Growth spurts and changes brought on by puberty occur during adolescence.

An adolescent may gain several inches in a few months, then experience very slow development for a while before experiencing another growth spurt.

Puberty (sexual maturation) changes can occur suddenly or gradually, depending on the individual.

The rate at which changes could occur can vary greatly.

These maturational indicators may appear for some youngsters earlier or later than for others.

What alterations will take place during puberty?

Hormonal changes cause the physical and sexual growth that occurs throughout puberty.
It might be challenging to predict the exact timing of puberty in guys.
Some changes take place, but they do so gradually and through time rather than all at once.
Although every male teenager is unique, the following are typical ages at which puberty changes may occur:

the age range for the onset of puberty: is 9.5 to 14

Testicular hypertrophy is the first pubertal alteration.

About a year after the testicles start to develop, the penis begins to enlarge.

Pubic hair appearance: 13.5 years old

Nocturnal emissions (sometimes known as "wet dreams"): 14

Age: 15, with facial and armpit hair, a different voice, and acne.

As a series of events, puberty also affects girls, but typically earlier than it does for boys their age.
Each girl is unique, so she may experience these changes differently.
The typical ages at which puberty changes may occur are as follows:

8 to 13 years old at the onset of puberty

The onset of breast growth during puberty

development of pubic hair: soon after breast development

Age in hair beneath the arms: 12

The age range for menstruation: is 10 to 16.5 years

When developing secondary sexual traits, both boys and girls go through particular developmental stages.

These physical traits—such as voice changes, body shapes, pubic hair distribution, and facial hair—distinguish between males and females and are unrelated to reproduction.

Here is a quick rundown of the modifications that take place:

The first signs of puberty in boys are an expansion of the scrotum and testicles.

The penis does not expand at this time.

The penis then lengthens as the testes and scrotum continue to grow.

The penis will then carry on expanding in both length and size.

The first sign of puberty in girls is the appearance of breast buds.

The breast and nipple will then rise.

At this period, the areola (the dark region of skin around the breast nipple) gets bigger.

The breasts then keep growing after that.

The areolas and nipples will eventually rise once more.
Another protrusion on the breasts is then formed.
Only the nipple is still raised above the rest of the breast tissue in the adult stage.

Both boys and girls experience similar pubic hair development.
When hair first grows, it only covers a limited region around the genitals and is long and soft.
Then, as it spreads, this hair gets darker and coarser.
Eventually, the pubic hair will resemble adult hair, but only in a limited area.
It could spread up the stomach occasionally and to the thighs.

What is my adolescent's comprehension?

Teenage years bring about a lot of changes, both physically and emotionally as well as socially.
Adolescents develop their capacity for abstract thought during this time, which helps them

eventually make plans and establish long-term objectives.
Every youngster develops at a different rate and has a unique perspective on the world.
Generally speaking, your adolescent may have some of the following skills:

increases the capacity for abstract thought

is interested in politics, philosophy, and social concerns.

makes comparisons with other people
Many changes may occur as your adolescent starts to fight for independence and authority.
Some of the problems that could arise with your adolescent throughout these years include the following:

Desires to be independent of parents

Peer approval and influence become crucial.

The importance of romantic and sexual relationships

possibly in love

Has committed to a long-term connection

How to support your adolescent's social development

Think about promoting your adolescent's social skills in the following ways:

Advise your teen to accept new challenges.

Talk to your adolescent about maintaining one's identity while interacting with others in a group.

Even if it's not you, you should encourage your adolescent to discuss issues or worries with a trustworthy adult.

Talk about stress management techniques.

Provide firm, loving discipline that includes boundaries, restraints, and rewards.

Chapter 4

Insinuations for understanding behavior

The conventional methods of discipline employed by parents when a child exhibits problematic behavior at home have relied on negative outcomes, such as punishment.
However, Positive Conduct Support (PBS) can offer a fresh perspective on how to approach and resolve hard situations brought on by challenging behavior.

The fact that negative consequences don't impart proper conduct is one of their key drawbacks.
Although punishment can instantly stop a child's bad behavior, it doesn't teach the youngster new skills to replace it with more fitting, constructive behavior.
In contrast to strategies based on unfavorable consequences, PBS emphasizes positive and instructional approaches.
The first and most crucial stage is to understand the child's behavior.

It is advised that parents pay close attention to challenging behavior in children and consider the meaning of the conduct because every behavior has a purpose.

Most of the time, a child's conduct acts as a means of communication, conveying to everyone the child's wants, sentiments, and physical condition.

The "function" of the problematic conduct refers to the message being conveyed by the child's behavior.

causes of behaviors

Behavior has a purpose and is a kind of communication.

behavior can be used to fulfill demands.

The top two requirements are:

to acquire - more time, clarity, organization, quiet, peer or adult attention, a desired object or activity, or sensory stimulation to avoid - a stressor, an irritant, a tough, boring, or easy task, a physical demand, an activity the student doesn't enjoy, or a peer.

When analyzing the causes of behavior, take into account:

environmental factors that can influence behavior, such as home, peers, friends, neighborhood, school practices, climate, socio-economic status, and the current point in time that may trigger the behavior - usual things outside the immediate environment. the developmental factors that may contribute to unwanted behavior - significant events that may have occurred previously in a child or young person's life.

Recognizing behaviors

Sometimes it can be challenging to comprehend a child's behavior choices.

However, it's crucial to realize that every action has a purpose.

Some people with impairments may only be able to express their needs or frustrations through conduct.

The behavioral guidelines that follow can help you understand how you can contribute.

Every action communicates something.
Everyone uses their conduct to communicate.
Similar to how an adult may yawn when he is bored at work, a baby may cry when she is hungry or damp.
Even if they are not aware of it, adults and children are always communicating something through their actions.
Problematic or improper behavior in children indicates that something is wrong and that the child is disturbed.

Problem behavior always has an explanation.
Children can have communication issues if they are unable to verbally articulate the issue or know what to do in a certain circumstance.

Children may act out their demands or sentiments during these moments.
Children display difficulty to conduct for a purpose.
There is always a rationale behind the behavior, whether it be to attract attention, cease an unpleasant activity, or satisfy sensory needs.

One particular behavior may have several causes.
Children who behave in a challenging way are communicating with adults that something is wrong or that their needs are not being met.
A single activity could have a variety of causes, including hunger, fear, pain, exhaustion, boredom, sadness, or anger.
Some kids may act in a way that seems detrimental just for the pleasure of the physical sensation (for example pulling threads from clothing).

Children sometimes act inappropriately when they feel unsafe or out of control, such as by kicking someone inappropriately.

Problem conduct is frequently used by a youngster to convey a very loud message to adults after making multiple attempts to express his demands but failing to do so.

Adults can learn to comprehend and interpret problematic behavior in youngsters.

Children frequently utilize their behavior to communicate what they need, so adults can assist the child by understanding the meaning behind the action.
Every child, but particularly those who exhibit problematic behavior, needs a consistent caring adult who will offer support and guidance, especially under trying circumstances.

Support, not punishment, can be used to lessen children's troublesome conduct.

Adults can react more effectively if they comprehend what messages youngsters are trying to convey through their conduct.

Children are less likely to engage in challenging conduct to express themselves when they feel appreciated and have their needs satisfied.

While punishing a child for behavior may temporarily halt it, it does not offer the child assistance or alternative strategies for responding to challenging circumstances.

Children gain vital social and problem-solving skills when adults assist them in finding constructive methods to express their needs to others. These skills will benefit them throughout their lives.

Chapter 5

How to Deal With Teenage Attitude

As a teen coach with years of experience, I frequently interact with parents who are dismayed by the attitude of their adolescents.
It might be difficult to know how to handle teenage attitudes.
While you don't want to make things worse, you also won't stand for disrespectful behavior.

Here are some things to keep in mind:

The attitude of your adolescent often has little to do with you.

Teenage years are challenging.
Teenagers are still feeling powerless and constrained by rules and schedules even if they are gaining a sense of who they are.
Although raising teenagers is never simple, there are simple things you can do right now to strengthen your bond with your children and communicate with them.

Seven approaches to address teenage attitude issues

It might be emotionally draining to try to understand your teen's difficult behavior, but this tried-and-true advice will help:

1. Only give counsel if your teen is receptive to it.

decent parenting abilities

It's difficult to watch your teenagers suffer with their issues as a parent, especially when you know you can assist.

After all, compared to your teens, you have a lot more life experience.

You could simply provide them with the remedies they require if they would only listen to you.

You want to help your teenagers succeed in school and have life-fulfilling lives.

However, they are still in the process of figuring out who they are.

They must establish their tastes and grow from their errors.

You can still direct and mentor your adolescent children if they are receptive to it.
But try your best to say less and listen more.
Even if you believe you know what's best for your teenagers, refrain from imposing your views on them.
If you listen to them instead of lecturing, they'll be more likely to express their opinions and feelings to you (without a negative attitude).

2. Establish firm boundaries with your teen.
Include your teenagers in the process of creating rules if you want them to respect boundaries.
They will realize that you regard and respect their thoughts and feelings if you act in this manner.
Now everyone in the household should find the rules to be reasonable.

Instead of letting your teenagers walk all over you, you're listening to their worries and establishing fair boundaries with them.

Make the rules as applicable to you (the parent) as feasible.

When the rules also apply to my wife and me, my children are more likely to follow them, at least in my own family.

Your teenagers will be far more inclined to follow rules that you establish together.

What's even better, though?

You won't have to worry about how to handle adolescent attitudes.

3. Allow your teen freedom.

Does it seem like only yesterday that your adolescent was a young child?

Do you recall the little kid that clung to you for everything and yearned for your company all the time?

You don't need me to tell you how fast kids grow up, therefore the task of developing mature adults begins right away.

Teenagers frequently experience the sense that their lives are beyond their control and that their independence is constantly being curtailed.
They are becoming more aware of who they are, but they frequently feel helpless.
This results in poor attitude and behavior.

Teenagers can't act right if they don't feel right, after all.
So wherever you can, give your teenagers some independence.
In exchange, you'll have more energy for the important things, even if it means making compromises on the little things (like your hairstyle or choice of clothing).
About the majority of decisions affecting their lives, such as which courses to take, which activities to engage in, and how to complete a project, teens should have the last say.

4. Remain composed during a mother-daughter argument

After dinner, you kindly request your daughter to do the dishes.
She slams her bedroom door after becoming irate and declaring that she doesn't want to.
As your annoyance grows, you reprimand her.
How else are you supposed to handle such an adolescent attitude?

Of course, being impolite or disrespectful is never appropriate.
Consequently, losing your temper will make your adolescent withdraw or become hostile.
It most certainly won't result in a fruitful discussion regarding your teen's inappropriate behavior.

Take a few deep breaths if you feel like you're ready to lose your cool.
Stay composed (here are some helpful hints for doing so) and, if necessary, talk to your kid about the situation once you both have calmed down.

5. Spend time with your adolescent.

Your adolescent children might not seem to want to hang out with you.
They can appear to find everything you do or say irritating.

The following should be kept in mind when dealing with teenage attitudes:

Even if they don't say it, your teens need your love and support.

If it seems that your other siblings, your job, or your hobbies are more important to you than they are, they could start to feel ignored.

They will behave worse if they feel this way.

Decide on a regular time to spend with your adolescent and make sure they are available throughout that period.

Take advantage of these chances to demonstrate your concern for your teen's interests and activities.

Both the parent-teen relationship and your teen's self-confidence and self-esteem will advance with time.

Quality time doesn’t have to be extravagant.

To show that you like spending time with your teen, all it takes is a neighborhood stroll or an afternoon spent getting ice cream.

Additionally, be careful not to lecture or badger your partner during this quality time; instead, it should be something you both look forward to.

6. Don't take a teenager's disrespectful actions personally

It's simple to feel that you're not managing the situation adequately when it comes to dealing with teenage attitudes.

You want to encourage your teenagers to assume personal responsibility so they can grow up to be successful, content adults.

But all your teenagers do is whine, argue with you, and challenge your authority.

It is helpful to keep in mind that their behavior often has less to do with you and more to do with the stage of growth they are in.
The way they think is evolving.
They are discovering who they are and learning how to communicate their heightened emotions.

That's a lot for a young child to handle!
Once more, I'm not advocating supporting inappropriate behavior.
It will be simpler to have a productive conversation with your teen once you realize that their attitude isn't a personal jab at you.
In turn, you have a better chance of getting your adolescent to pay attention to you.

7. Increase your teen's self-assurance
You want to foster good lifelong habits in your teenagers.
You then make a constructive suggestion.
You advise your teenagers to study more, keep their rooms tidy, eat healthily, and limit their screen time.

Don't forget to compliment your teenagers when you're working to help them develop greater responsibility!

Recognizing teens' good behavior encourages moral development and identity construction.
Instead of using evaluative praise, I advise using descriptive praise.
(Some examples of elaborative laud are provided here.)

You'll encourage positive behavior, increase your teens' self-confidence, and promote long-lasting success-oriented habits by doing this. Your home will be more peaceful, which will mean fewer fights between you and your teenagers.

www.ingramcontent.com/pod-product-compliance
Lightning Source LLC
LaVergne TN
LVHW052104160826
845678LV00015B/3359

* 9 7 9 8 8 4 6 0 9 9 3 3 3 *